D0975462

SUCK ON THIS YEAR

LYFAO @ 140 Characters or Less

Denis Leary

VIKING

VIKING
Published by the Penguin Group
Penguin Group (USA) Inc., 375 Hudson Street,
New York, New York 10014, U.S.A.
Penguin Group (Canada), 90 Eglinton Avenue East, Suite 700,
Toronto, Ontario, Canada M4P 2Y3
(a division of Pearson Penguin Canada Inc.)
Penguin Books Ltd, 80 Strand, London WC2R 0RL, England
Penguin Ireland, 25 St. Stephen's Green, Dublin 2, Ireland
(a division of Penguin Books Ltd)
Penguin Books Australia Ltd, 250 Camberwell Road, Camberwell,
Victoria 3124, Australia
(a division of Pearson Australia Group Pty Ltd)
Penguin Books India Pvt Ltd, 11 Community Centre, Panchsheel Park,
New Delhi – 110 017, India
Penguin Group (NZ), 67 Apollo Drive, Rosedale, North Shore 0632,
New Zealand (a division of Pearson New Zealand Ltd)
Penguin Books (South Africa) (Pty) Ltd, 24 Sturdee Avenue,
Rosebank, Johannesburg 2196, South Africa

Penguin Books Ltd, Registered Offices:
80 Strand, London WC2R 0RL, England

First published in 2010 by Viking Penguin,
a member of Penguin Group (USA) Inc.

10   9   8   7   6   5   4   3   2   1

Photographs courtesy of AFP/Getty Images; AP/Wide World Photos;
Martin Bureau/AFP/Getty Images; M. Caulfield/WireImage/Getty
Images; Corbis Images; Everett Collection, Inc.; FotoArena/LatinContent
Editorial/Getty Images; iStockphoto; Amy Sussman/WireImage/Getty
Images; and X17, Inc. Some of the images have been altered for satirical
purposes.

ISBN 978-0-670-02289-2

Printed in the United States of America
Interior design by The Molecule

Introduction

My wife was an early addition to the Twitter universe. And about four seconds after her first experience she began chiding me about how I should join up. Of course - due to my naturally rebellious nature - I said no. Only because that's my first reaction whenever someone tells me to do something - I do the opposite. A cop says the road is closed? I drive down it. Fast. A nun says masturbation will make you go blind? I buy sunglasses, a cane and all the dirty magazines I can get my hungry hands on.

And so it was with Tweeter (which was my first derogatory term for it). It seemed to be filled with people sending people to other people's tweet places to read articles about How To Keep Your Kids From Selling Oxycontin and Why Barack Obama Really Isn't Black and What Bikini Waxing Works Best and blah blah blah.

Then Ann told me there were famous people using this new technology. That's when I started referring to it as Twatter.

Just what the world needs: famously vapid assheads twatting about expensive designer watches they got for free in swag bags while attending The First Annual Watkins Glen Film Festival and posting TwatPics of themselves with celebutard sunburns and Courtney Love bitch-twatting everyone on earth including her own daughter with spelling so bad it makes Paris Hilton look like Stephen Fucking Hawking.

I don't have anything to Twunt about on a daily basis.

I wake up, I drink coffee, I watch SportsCenter.

Then I read the papers online and make wise-ass remarks to myself.

And then I go to work.

That's when it hit me.

At work some of the guys and girls will mention something in the news and I'll repeat one of the wise-ass things I said to myself earlier. Or someone will make a wise-ass comment of their own about anything - Heidi Montag's fake ass or Danny Trejo's real face or gay marriage or secretly gay politicians railing against gay marriage - and I'll add something new of my own and we'll all laugh. Sometimes a lot.

And unless I'm going on a stand-up comedy tour or getting ready for an appearance on Letterman or have a charity gig coming up - I never use any of this stuff. It just happens and disappears.

So I said to one of the guys I work with, hey - maybe I should give this Twat thing a try. Nah - I don't think it's for you. You don't do anything that's really Twat-worthy. You're a BORING celebrity. That stuff's for celebrities who get shitfaced and fall down and get arrested and hang out with other celebrities and have celebrity beefs and go to parties and are married to other celebrities. Lady Gaga and Kim Kardashian and Demi Moore and Ashton Kutcher.

That was all I had to hear. Lady Gaga and the Kardashian Klan and all these other people - I make jokes about these guys every time I see a picture of them. That's my job.

Because underneath all the Emmy-losing acting performances and the Emmy-losing scripts I write and the Oscar-ignored films I produce and sometimes star in (once with an elephant) beats the raging heart of a comedy bull.

So I started to Tweet. And once I started, I couldn't stop. And once I couldn't stop I tried to figure out a way to make money off all of it. Thus - this book. Or mini-book. Or celebrity coaster. A portion of the proceeds from this glorified pamphlet with pictures will go towards my charity - The Leary Firefighters Foundation. So not only are you probably improving your own life by buying this and reading it (which should only take about 20 minutes) and hopefully laughing out loud - you are also helping a firefighter somewhere in America gain some invaluable training in a new or improved facility or placing a needed piece of equipment into his or her hands.

So thanks for that.

And let's be honest - if you just received this as a Xmas present - it's a fuck of a lot more fun than those new winter socks or that stupid goddamn sweater or most of your relatives.

Now - read, laugh and blow eggnog out of your nose. Or laugh so hard you puke. That's what I love about comedy. It makes noises and fluids come flying out of your body. Which has to be a good thing, right?

Love and kisses,

Denis.

P.S. Special Thanks to my wife Ann and our two hilarious kids Jack and Devin. Not for anything in particular on this project. Just because they have made my life so fall down funny and outrageously exciting for the last twenty years.

P.P.S. Extra Special Thanks to Jim Serpico, Bill Scheft, Ken Rogerson, Paul Masella, Tom Sellitti, Bartow Church, Lydia Wills, Clare Ferraro, Josh Kendall, Carolyn Coleburn and The Molecule for their ideas and inspiration and without whom this book never would have happened.

P.P.P.S. Extra EXTRA Special Thanks to Sarah Palin, Glenn Beck, Paris Hilton, Lady Gaga and Iran. I must get at least three tweet ideas a week from these popular entities. Keep the crazy comments coming guys.

P.P.P.P.S. Go Sox.

SUCK ON THIS YEAR

LYFAO @ 140 Characters or Less

Twitter is about to announce a new pay model.

For 25 bucks a month you never hear from Ashton Kutcher again.

To celebrate Earth Day I spent three hours picking up trash.

Started to feel a little bit like Jesse James.

Scientists create new embryo that's one part man, two parts woman.

Calling it marriage.

Laura Bush says she and President poisoned during a meal in 2007.

Well, you eat enough shit - there's bound to be something bad in it.

This just in:

Vatican acquires Neverland Ranch.

Behavior Test: Flamboyant male dancing attracts most women.

And men who love show tunes.

Company sued for tampon found in cereal.

Maybe the prizes are just getting more practical.

Lindsay Lohan to play Linda Lovelace in pornstar biopic.

Exactly whose reputation is at stake here?

Arizona residents: "we're sick of being called racists."

That's the thing about Arizona:
it's a dry hate.

Lettuce recalled in 23 states.

Experts fear it could affect up to 5 Americans.

Pope admits: Church has sinned.

In other news: Bear shits in woods.

Elena Kagan would become 3rd Jewish Supreme Court Justice.

May mean nothing to you but it's killing Mel Gibson.

Sarah Palin.

Excellent argument for
separation of church and brain.

Larry King puts his divorce on hold.

And another one on marriage forwarding.

Woman hits on Obama in Buffalo NY wing joint.

Prez does right thing.
Gives her Clinton's number.

The Pope is against gay marriage.

This coming from a grown man who goes to work dressed like Lady Gaga.

Warrant goes out for Lindsay Lohan's arrest.

Authorities warn that both parents are still at large.

New Jersey worried about oil residue on beaches.

Not from Gulf spill.
From cast of Jersey Shore.

Floyd Landis implicates Lance Armstrong in steroid scandal.

Takes a lot of balls.
Three to be exact.

2 yr old Indonesian boy has 2 pack a day smoking habit.

Pussy.

Study: heavy girls have sex earlier.

And a sandwich.

Study: younger siblings take higher and much more dangerous risks.

I'm praying there's not a
Betty Winehouse.

World Cup Stat: Team Argentina docs will allow players to have sex during tournament.

They just can't use their hands.

FBI releases list of Ted Kennedy death threats.

Not surprisingly, over half were written on cocktail napkins.

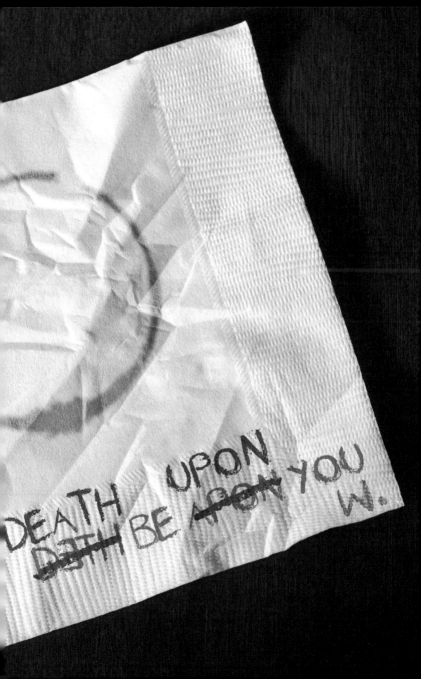

Survey: 1 in 5 high school students have abused prescription drugs.

The other 4 are no fun at all.

10,000 priests gather in Rome to listen to Pope.

And kids drink free!

Study: Extroverted men, neurotic women are the most fertile.

Seriously, is that a study, or the synopsis for "John and Kate, Plus 8?"

39

Lebron goes to Miami.

Cleveland announces
Going Out Of Business Sale.

Cheney gets heart pump implant.

Lets all pray it's made by BP.

Study:
Obese people
have decreased
mental acuity.

But incredible focus on pies.

Judge:
Wesley Snipes
must spend 3 years
in jail.

Not for tax evasion. The Blade trilogy.

I didn't get nominated for a 2010 Emmy but the guy who extorted Letterman did.

Wow. Next year I'm gonna kidnap Regis.

Vatican revises rule on clergy sex abuse:

kids now get a 5 second head start.

Report: Britain tortured its own people.

Hey - join the club. Keeping Up With The Kardashians is entering season four.

Doctors: attention deficit disorder can destroy a marriage.

I think I speak for all husbands when I say: 'You seen my keys?'

Report: Jews and Agnostics have 20% more sex than Catholics.

Unless you count bishops and priests. Then it's no contest.

NFL considering use of tracking microchip inside ball.

How about putting one in Ben Rapelisberger's cock?

Naomi Campbell: I didn't know dirty-looking stones were diamonds.

Which is why she winged them at the maid.

Michael Jackson Casino opens online.

You can only make bets with hush money.

Avg. American drinks 4 cases of beer, 12 bottles of wine and 2 qrts of liquor a year.

At my Uncle Sean's house we call that Friday night.

Salmonella fear leads to recall of 380 million eggs.

I'm praying that Snooki's are included.

Paris Hilton on coke charge: it wasn't my purse.

Yeah, right. And in the video it wasn't her vagina.

Study: nasty people have more heart attacks.

Cheney's had five. Case closed.

Octomom to DWTS: I was born to dance!

Hey - if she had any rhythm,
she wouldn't have 14 Octokids.

Lady Gaga: drugs inspired me.

Yeah, we know - we've seen the outfits.

Indonesia's smoking toddler finally kicks habit.

It got easier once he quit drinking.

New DNA test shows Hitler had Jewish, African blood.

And I thought Mel Gibson was having a bad year.

Paris Hilton says she thought bag of cocaine was gum.

Who's her lawyer - Roger Clemens?

Study says heavy drinkers live 9% longer than teetotalers.

And have 99.9% more cases of whiskey dick.

Health study: owning a dog cuts child obesity rate by 50%.

25% if the kid eats the pet.

Britney Spears sued for sexual harassment by ex-bodyguard.

Big deal. When is she gonna let her baby drive the car again?

Experts: best time for sex is 7 a.m.

Unless she wakes up.

Scientists discover traces of water on asteroid.

Call me when they find scotch.

Ben Rapelisberger suspended for six games by NFL.

Two for the alleged assault - five for the mullet.

Lady Gaga says she's celibate right now.

No shit. Hard to have sex with someone who's wearing a plastic house.

Heidi Montag has 10 plastic surgeries in one day.

Experts believe if she stays healthy she may pass Melissa Rivers by the All-Star break.

Jessica Simpson says she only brushes her teeth 3 times a week.

Guess she gets too dizzy moving her head from side to side.

Arizona passes law against ethnic studies.

How long before Arizona just says "Screw it - we're invading Poland"

'Situation' signs book deal – will release 'Here's The Situation' in the fall.

What will take you longer to read – that book or this tweet?

Art Linkletter, Dennis Hopper and Gary Coleman.

Looks like heaven is done casting
Two and a Half Men.

Cheney out of intensive care and in great form.

Plans to resume fishing, shooting people in the face and pillaging the earth ASAP.

Steinbrenner fires God

- replaces him with Bob Lemon.

Judge overturns ban on same sex marriage in California.

Ticking sounds begin to emerge from inside Glenn Beck's head.

Mexican gov't considers legalizing pot.

Finally, a reason to sneak IN to Mexico.

Keith Richards hasn't had a drink in 14 weeks.

Big Deal. Charlie Watts hasn't uttered a sound since 1987.

Ron Wood mistook white cookies for crack.

Lucky for him. Remember when
Brian Jones mistook his pool for a sofa?

Report: Amish population seems to be increasing.

So much for the effectiveness of wood condoms.

Paris Hilton pleads guilty to cocaine charge.

And possession of Lindsay Lohan's phone number.

Liotta, Ray

Lohan, Lindsay

Loken, Kristanna

Lindsay Lohan
VP Founder Cokelets

UNEMPLOYE
LVL 8
$0

JOB
WANTE

MICHAEL
JACKSON:
THE EXPERIENCE

Michael Jackson video game will not be easy.

Level 8 involves finding work for Tito.

Marijuana growers join teamsters union:

Finally a dealer who delivers.

.